TOM PETTY
FOR UKULELE

ISBN 978-1-4950-7175-1

7777 W. BLUEMOUND RD. P.O. BOX 13819 MILWAUKEE, WI 53213

Visit Hal Leonard Online at
www.halleonard.com

American Girl

Words and Music by Tom Petty

Yeah, and if she had to die tryin', she _____

God, it's so pain - ful when some - thin' that's so close _____

had one lit - tle prom - ise she was gon - na keep. _____

is still so far out _ of reach. _____

Chorus

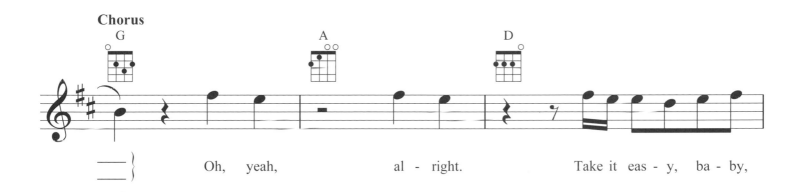

Oh, yeah, al - right. Take it eas - y, ba - by,

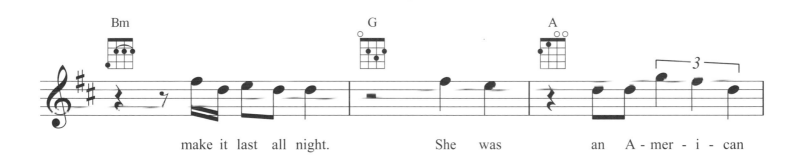

make it last all night. She was an A - mer - i - can

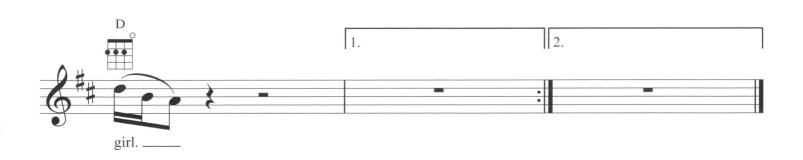

girl. _____

Breakdown

Words and Music by Tom Petty

Go a-head, give __ it to me. Break down, hon-ey; take __

__ me through __ the night. __ Break down, now I'm

stand-in' here, can't you see? __ Break down, it's all

right, __ it's all right,

it's all right.

Don't Come Around Here No More

Words and Music by Tom Petty and David Stewart

Verse
Slowly, with a beat

1. Don't come a - round here no more. ___
2. I don't feel ___ you an - y - more, ___

Don't come a - round here no more. ___
you dark - en my door. ___

What - ev - er you're look - ing for, ___

(Hey!) don't come a - round here no more. ___

Chorus

I've giv - en up. (Stop.) I've giv - en up. (Stop.)

I've giv-en up (stop) on wait-ing an-y long - er.
I've giv-en up. (Stop.) You tan - gle my e - mo - tions.

I've giv-en up on this love _____ get - ting strong - er. _____
I've giv-en up. Hon - ey, please, _____ ad - mit it's o - ver. _____

1.
Don't come a - round here no more. _____

Don't come a - round here no more. _____

Don't come a - round here no more. _____

Don't come a - round here no more. _____

9

Don't come a-round here no more. ___

Don't come a-round here no more. ___ Stop walk-ing down ___ my

street. Don't come a-round here no more. ___

Who do you ___ ex-pect to meet? Don't come a-round here no more. ___

___ And what-ev-er you're look-ing for,

(Hey!) don't come a-round here no more. ___

Free Fallin'

Words and Music by Tom Petty and Jeff Lynne

Verse

long day ____ liv - in' in Re - se - da. There's a

(3., 4.) *See additional lyrics*

free - way ____ run - nin' through the yard. ____ And I'm a

bad boy ____ 'cause I don't e - ven miss ____ her. I'm a

bad boy ____ for break - in' her ____ heart. ____ And I'm

Chorus

free, free fall - in'.

Yeah, I'm free, free

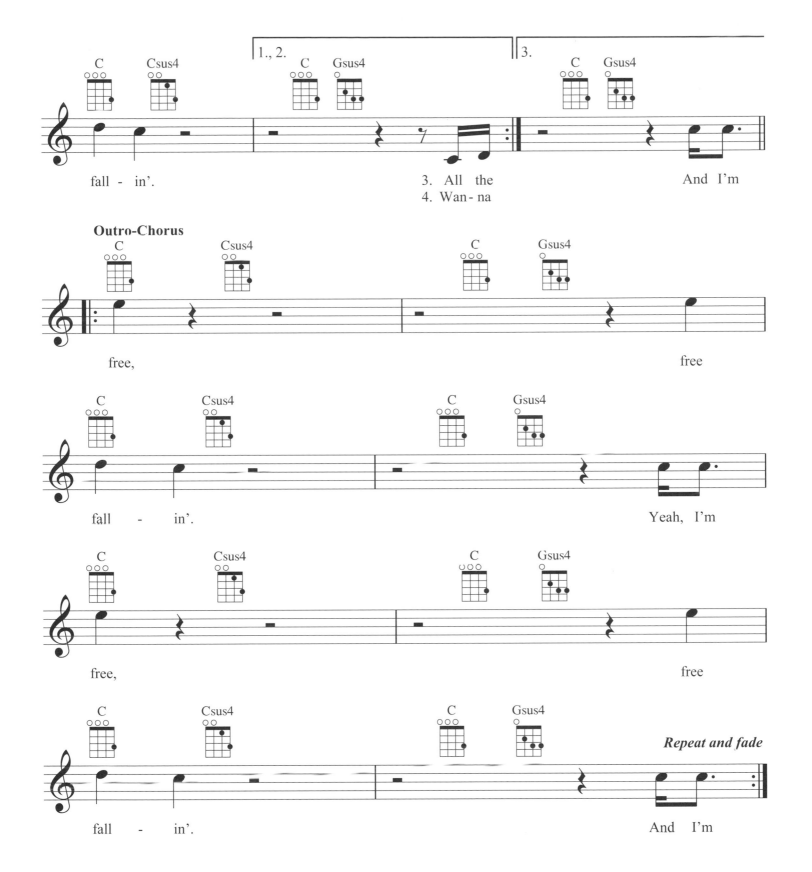

Additional Lyrics

3. All the vampires walkin' through the valley
   Move west down Ventura Boulevard.
   And all the bad boys are standing in the shadows,
   And the good girls are home with broken hearts.

4. Wanna glide down over Mulholland.
   I wanna write her name in the sky.
   I wanna free fall out into nothin'.
   Gonna leave this world for a while.

Don't Do Me Like That

Words and Music by Tom Petty

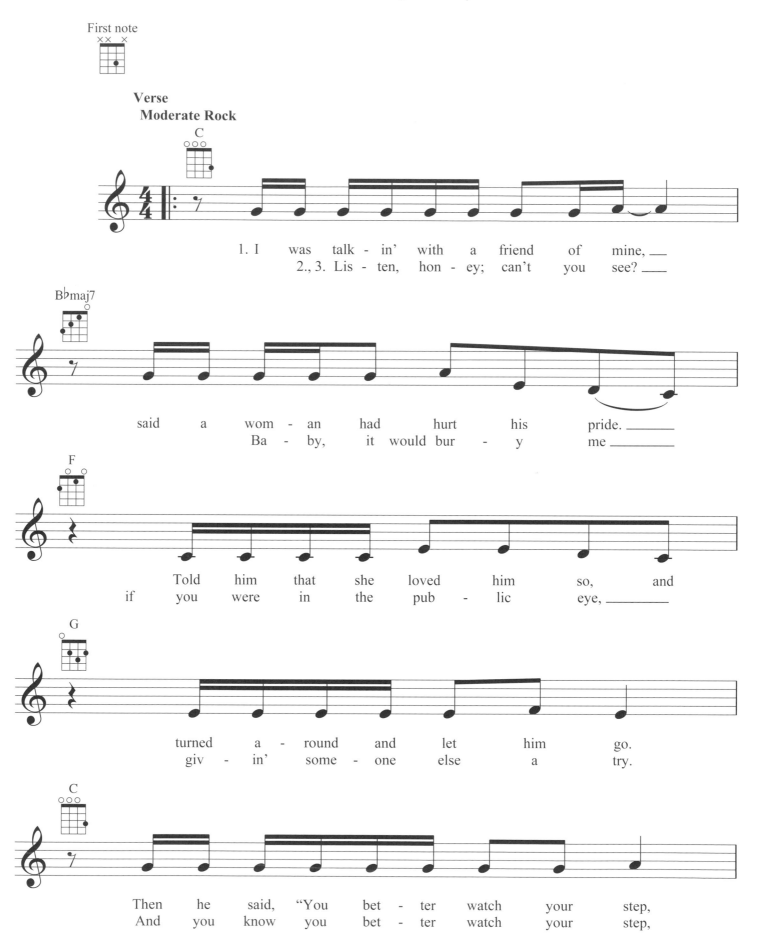

First note

Verse
Moderate Rock

1. I was talk - in' with a friend of mine, ___
2., 3. Lis - ten, hon - ey; can't you see? ___

said a wom - an had hurt his pride. ___
Ba - by, it would bur - y me ___

Told him that she loved him so, and
if you were in the pub - lic eye, ___

turned a - round and let him go.
giv - in' some - one else a try.

Then he said, "You bet - ter watch your step,
And you know you bet - ter watch your step,

14

2.

Am ... F ... G

What if I need you, ba - by? Don't do me like that, 'cause

Bridge

C7 ... F

some - where deep down in - side, ___ some - one is say - in', "Love ___

C7 ... F

___ does - n't last ___ that ___ long." ___

C7 ... F

I've had this feel - in' in - side ___ night out and day ___ in, and,

Fm ... G ... *D.C. al Coda*

ba - by, I can't take ___ it no more. ___

Coda

Am ... F ... G ... C

I just might need you, hon - ey. Don't do me like that.

Into the Great Wide Open

Words and Music by Tom Petty and Jeff Lynne

First note

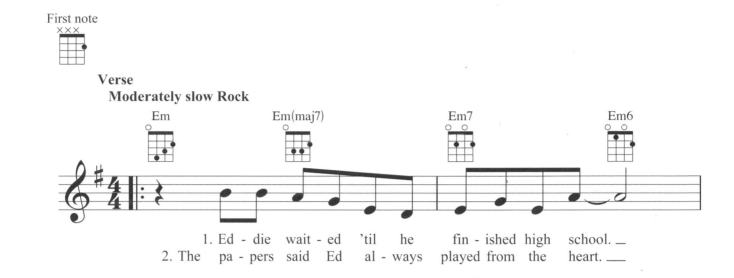

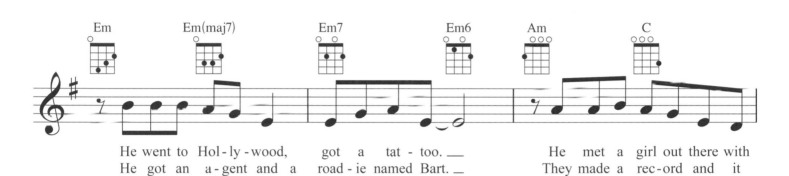

1. Ed - die wait - ed 'til he fin - ished high school. ___
2. The pa - pers said Ed al - ways played from the heart. ___

He went to Hol - ly - wood, got a tat - too. ___ He met a girl out there with
He got an a - gent and a road - ie named Bart. _ They made a rec - ord and it

a tat - too, too. ___ The fu - ture was wide o - pen. ___
went in the charts. _ The sky was the lim - it. _____

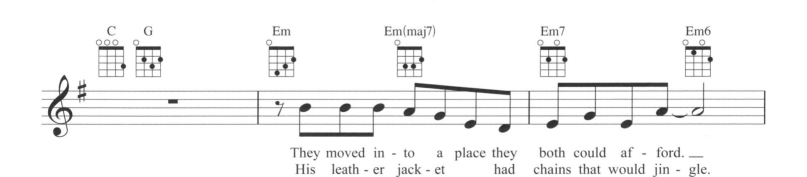

They moved in - to a place they both could af - ford. ___
His leath - er jack - et had chains that would jin - gle.

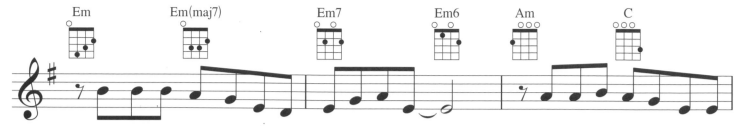

He found a night-club; he could work at the door. ___ She had a gui-tar and she
They both met mov-ie stars, par-tied and min-gled. Their A and R man said, "I

taught him some chords. ___ The sky was ___ the lim-it. _____ }
don't hear a sin-gle." The fu-ture was wide ___ o-pen. _____ }

Chorus

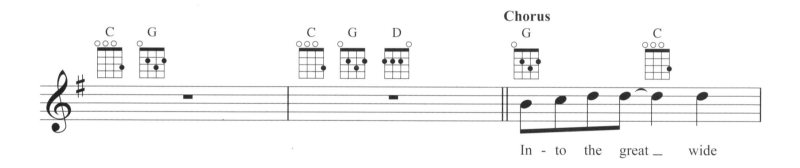

In-to the great ___ wide

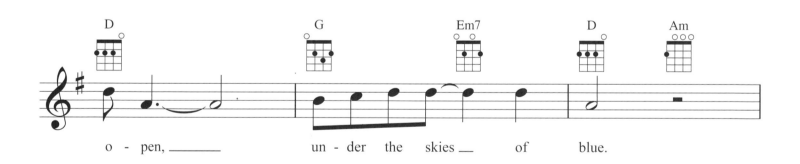

o-pen, _____ un-der the skies ___ of blue.

Out in the great ___ wide o-pen, _____ a reb-el with-out ___ a clue. ___

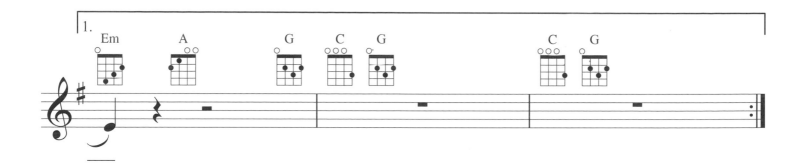

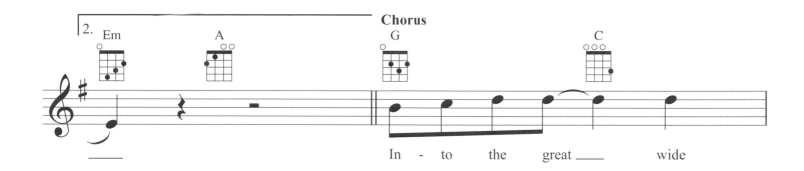

Chorus

In - to the great ___ wide

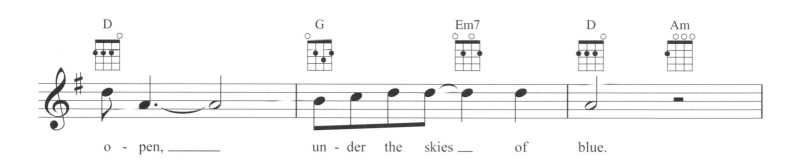

o - pen, ___ un - der the skies ___ of blue.

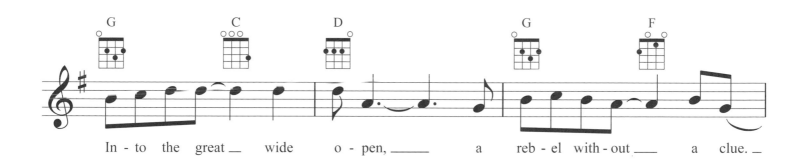

In - to the great ___ wide o - pen, ___ a reb - el with - out ___ a clue. ___

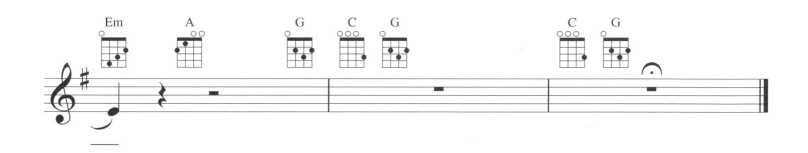

I Won't Back Down

Words and Music by Tom Petty and Jeff Lynne

Learning to Fly

Words and Music by Tom Petty and Jeff Lynne

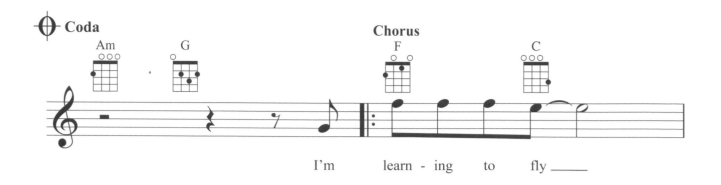

Coda

Chorus

I'm learn - ing to fly ____

but I ain't got wings. ___
a - round the clouds. ___

Com - ing down ___ is the
What goes up ____

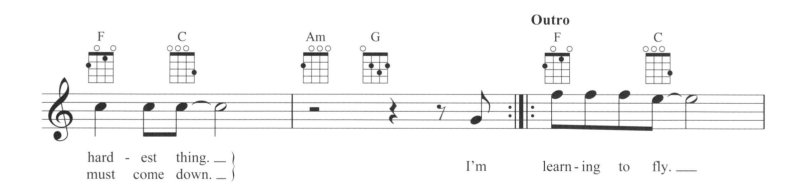

Outro

hard - est thing. _)
must come down. _)

I'm learn - ing to fly. ___

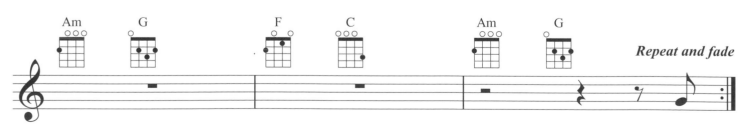

Repeat and fade

I'm

Runnin' Down a Dream

Words and Music by Tom Petty, Jeff Lynne and Mike Campbell

First note

Bright Rock

Verse

1. It was a beau-ti-ful day, _____ the
(2.) felt so good, _____ like an -
3. I rolled on, _____ the

sun beat down.   I had the ra-di-o on;
-y-thing was pos-si-ble.   Hit cruise con-trol
sky grew dark.   I put the ped-al down

I was driv-in'.
and rubbed my eyes. _____
to make some time. _____

The
The
There's

trees went by.
last three days
some-thing good

Me and Del were sing-in'
the rain _____ was un-stop-pa-ble.
wait-in' down this road. _____

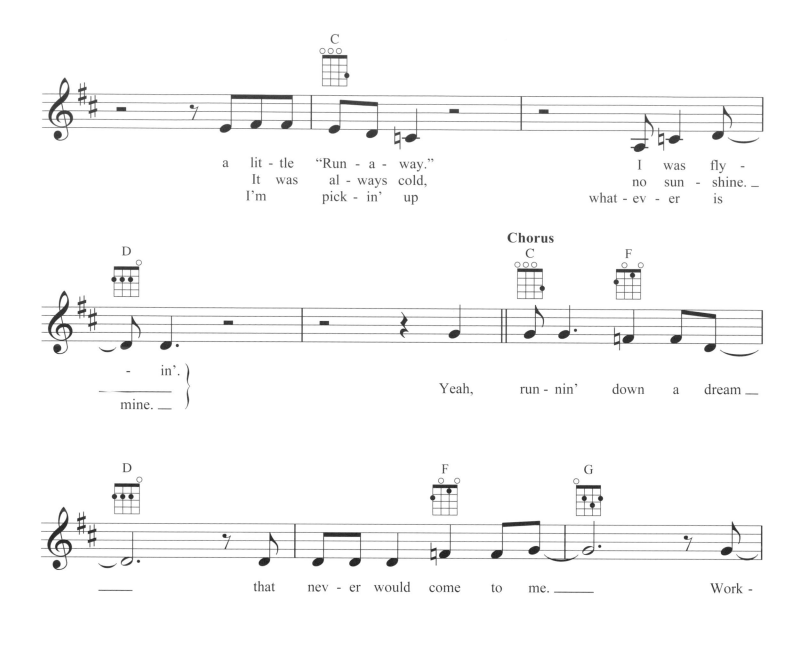

a lit - tle "Run - a - way."
It was al - ways cold,
I'm pick - in' up

I was fly -
no sun - shine. __
what - ev - er is

Chorus

- in'.
mine. __

Yeah, run - nin' down a dream __

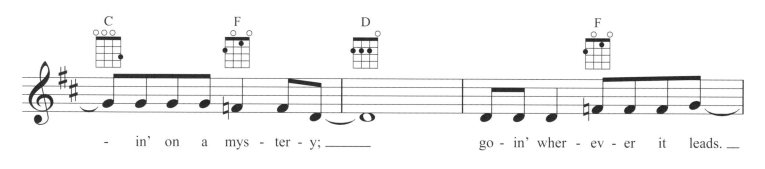

__ that nev - er would come to me. ___ Work -

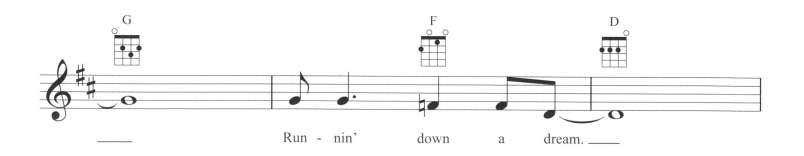

- in' on a mys - ter - y; _____ go - in' wher - ev - er it leads. __

__ Run - nin' down a dream. ____

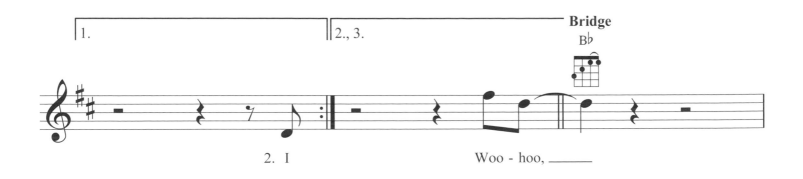

2. I

Bridge

Woo - hoo, _____

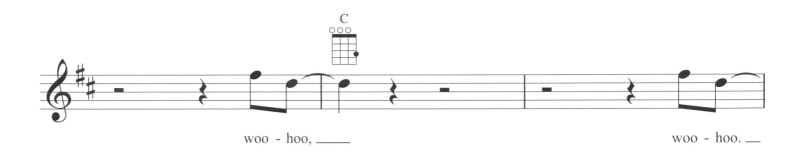

woo - hoo, _____   woo - hoo. _

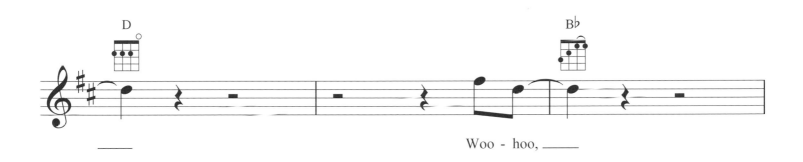

_____   Woo - hoo, _____

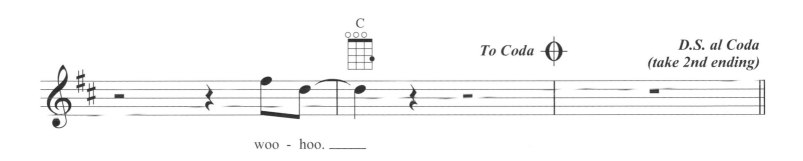

woo - hoo. _____   *D.S. al Coda (take 2nd ending)*

Woo - hoo.

Mary Jane's Last Dance

Words and Music by Tom Petty

First note

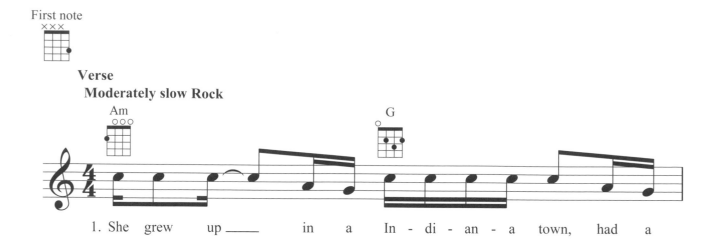

Verse
Moderately slow Rock

1. She grew up _____ in a In - di - an - a town, had a

good - look - in' ma - ma who nev - er was a - round. But she

grew up tall ___ and she grew up right ___ with them In - di - an - a boys on an In - di - an - a night.

Verse

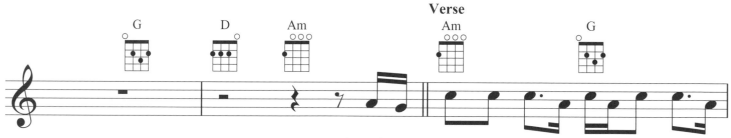

2. Well, she moved down here the age of eight - een. She

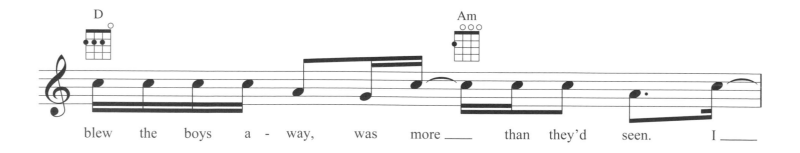

blew the boys a - way, was more _____ than they'd seen. I ___

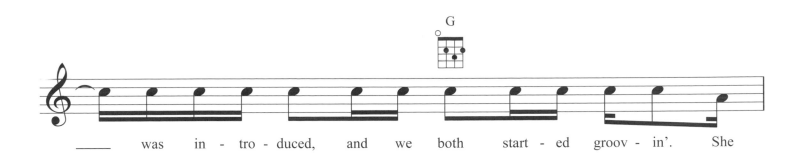

was in - tro - duced, and we both start - ed groov - in'. She

said, "I dig you, ba - by, but I got to keep mov - in' on." ___

Chorus

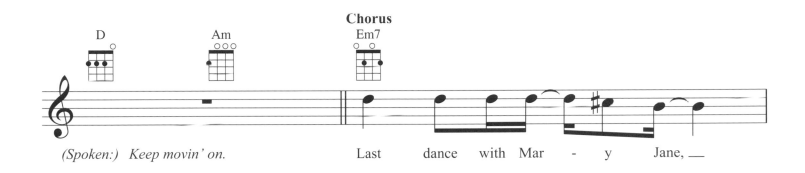

(Spoken:) Keep movin' on.   Last dance with Mar - y Jane, ___

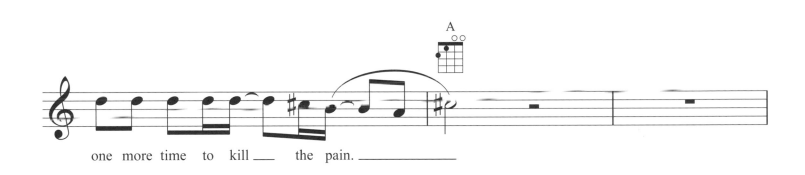

one more time to kill ___ the pain. ___

I feel sum - mer creep - in' in, ___ and I'm   tired ___ of this town a - gain. ___

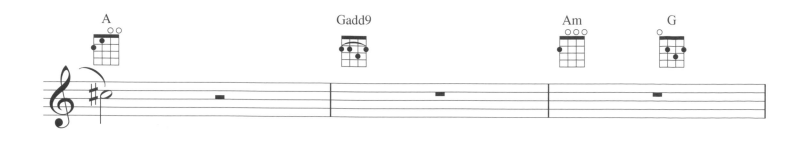

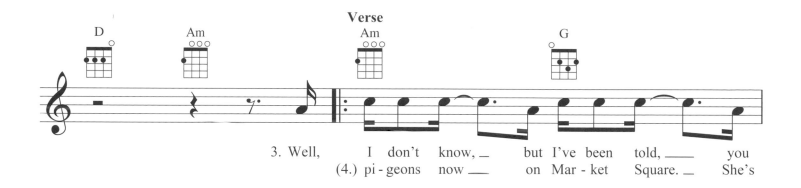

3. Well, I don't know, __ but I've been told, ____ you
(4.) pi - geons now __ on Mar - ket Square. __ She's

nev - er slow down, you nev - er grow old. Tired of screw - in' up, __ tired __ of go - in' down, tired _
stand - in' in her un - der - wear, look - in' down _ from a ho - tel _ room; __ and

____ of my - self, tired __ of this town. Oh my my, oh ____ hell yes,
night - fall will be com - ing __ soon. Oh my my, oh ____ hell yes, you

hon - ey, put on ____ that par - ty dress. __ Buy me a drink, sing me a song,
got to put on ____ that par - ty dress. __ It was too cold to cry when I woke up a - lone. I

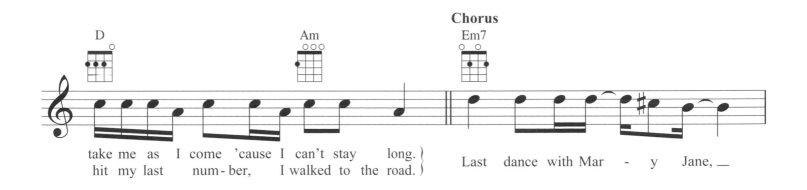

take me as I come 'cause I can't stay long. ⎫
hit my last num-ber, I walked to the road. ⎭

Chorus

Last dance with Mar - y Jane, __

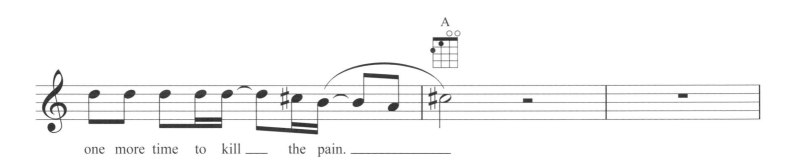

one more time to kill __ the pain. __

I feel sum-mer creep-in' in, __ and I'm tired __ of this town a - gain. __

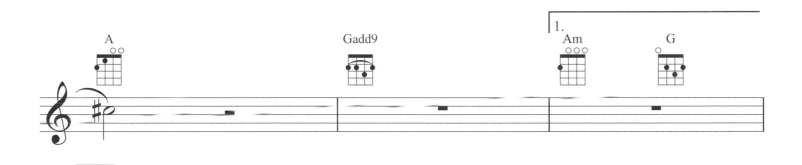

4. There's

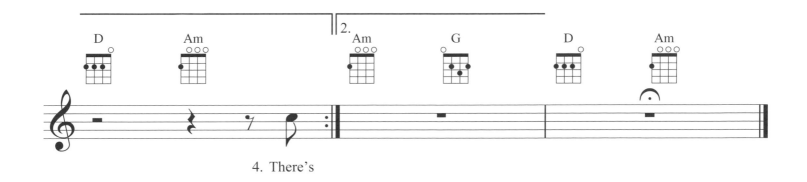

31

Refugee

Words and Music by Tom Petty and Mike Campbell

First note

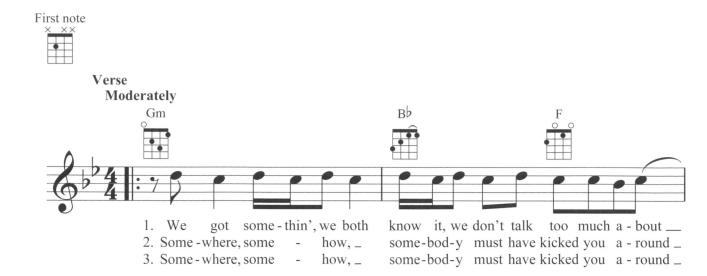

1. We got some-thin', we both know it, we don't talk too much a-bout ___
2. Some-where, some - how, _ some-bod-y must have kicked you a-round _
3. Some-where, some - how, _ some-bod-y must have kicked you a-round _

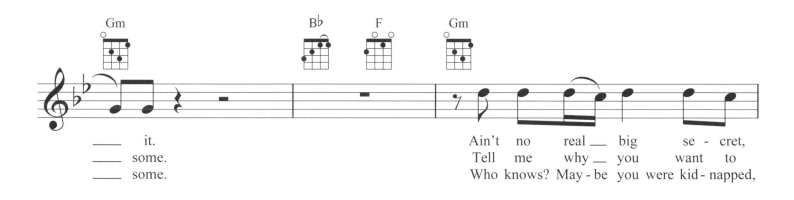

___ it.   Ain't no real ___ big se - cret,
___ some.   Tell me why _ you want to
___ some.   Who knows? May - be you were kid - napped,

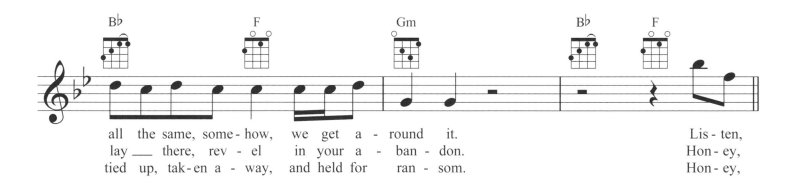

all the same, some-how, we get a - round it.   Lis - ten,
lay ___ there, rev - el in your a - ban - don.   Hon - ey,
tied up, tak-en a - way, and held for ran - som.   Hon - ey,

Pre-Chorus

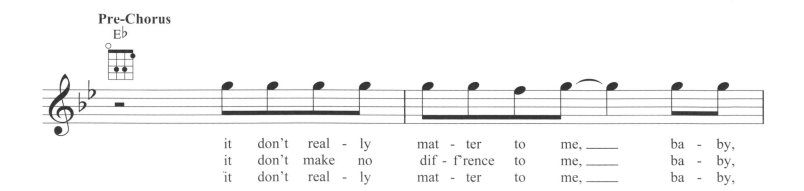

it don't real - ly mat - ter to me, ___ ba - by,
it don't make no dif - f'rence to me, ___ ba - by,
it don't real - ly mat - ter to me, ___ ba - by,

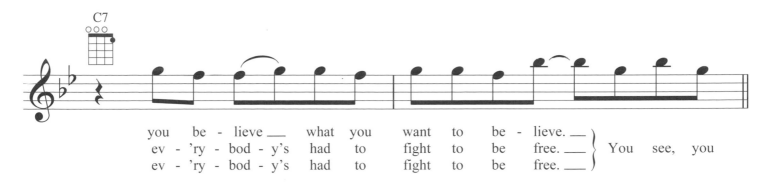

you be - lieve ___ what you want to be - lieve. ___
ev - 'ry - bod - y's had to fight to be free. ___ } You see, you
ev - 'ry - bod - y's had to fight to be free. ___

Chorus

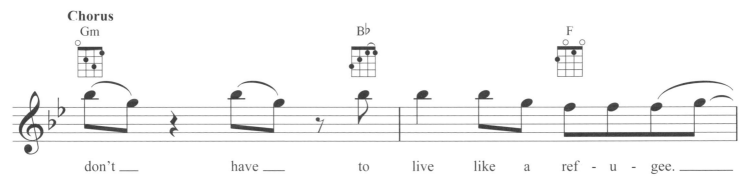

don't ___ have ___ to live like a ref - u - gee. _____

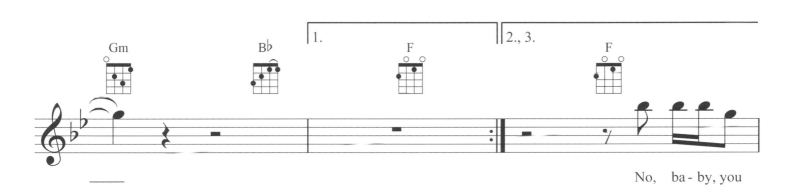

1. 2., 3.

___ No, ba - by, you

To Coda ⊕

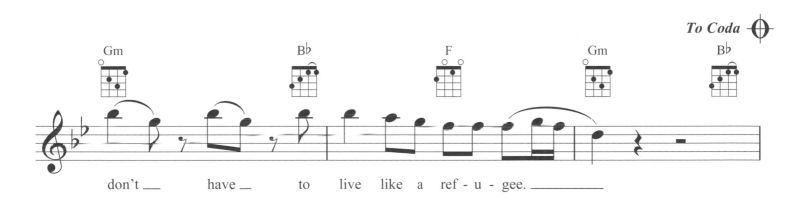

don't ___ have ___ to live like a ref - u - gee. _____

Bridge

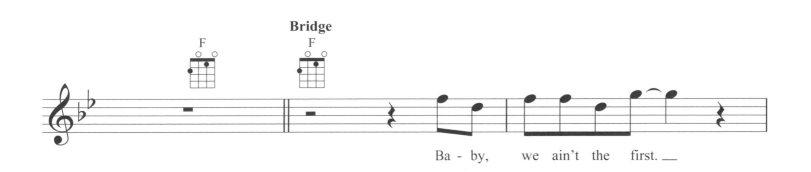

Ba - by, we ain't the first. ___

33

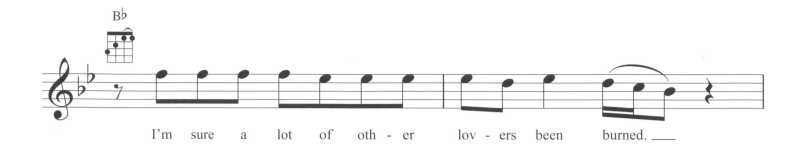

I'm sure a lot of oth - er lov - ers been burned. ____

Right now this seems real ____ to you, ____ but it's

D.C. al Coda
(take 2nd ending)

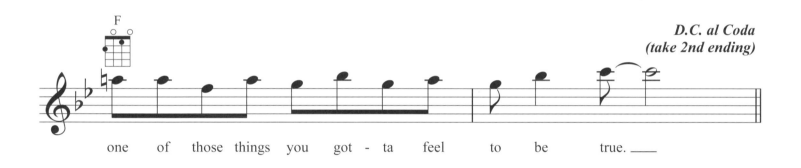

one of those things you got - ta feel to be true. ____

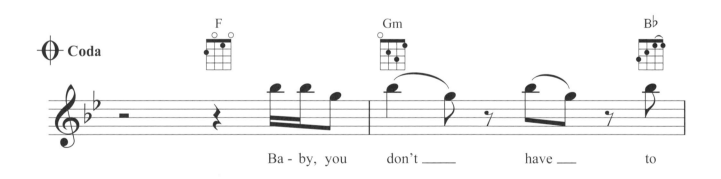

Ba - by, you don't ____ have ____ to

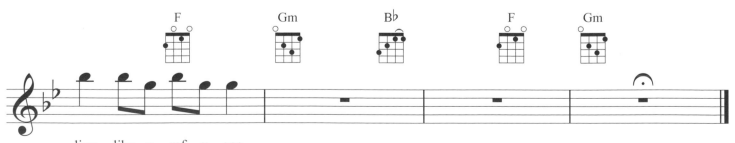

live like a ref - u - gee.

Stop Draggin' My Heart Around

Words and Music by Tom Petty and Mike Campbell

1. Ba - by, you'll come knock-ing on my ___ front door.

Same old line you used to use be - fore. I said, "Yeah." ___ Well, ___

what am I s'posed to do? I did - n't know ___ what I was

get - ting in - to. So you've had a lit - tle

trou - ble in town. ___ Now you're keep - ing some

de - mon down. ___ Stop drag - gin' my, stop drag - gin' my,

stop drag - gin' my heart a - round.

Verse

2. It's hard to think a - bout what you've want - ed.
3. There's peo - ple run - ning 'round loose in the world

It's hard to think a - bout what you've lost.
ain't got ___ noth - ing bet - ter to do,

This does - n't have to be the big get e - ven.
make a meal of some bright - eyed kid. ___

Em   G   A

This does-n't have to be ____ an - y - thing at all. ⎫
You need some - one look-ing af - ter ____ you. ⎭

Em   G   A

I know you real - ly want to tell me good - bye.

Chorus

Em   G   A   C

I know you real - ly want to be your own girl.   Ba - by, you could nev - er

D   C

look me in the eye. ____   Yeah, you buck - le with the

D   C   D

weight of the words. __   Stop drag - gin' my,   stop drag - gin' my,

C   G   C   Em

stop drag - gin' my heart a - round.

Walls
(Circus)
Words and Music by Tom Petty

First note

1. Some days are dia - monds. Some days are rocks. __
2. *See additional lyrics*

__ Some doors are o - pen.

Some roads are blocked. __ Sun - downs __ are gold -
3. *See additional lyrics*

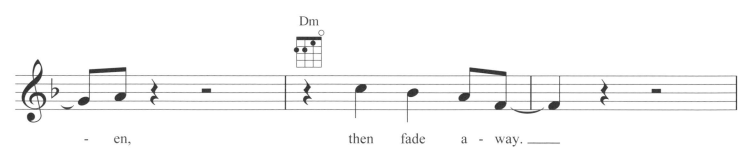

- en, then fade a - way. ____

And if I nev - er do noth - in', I'll get you back some -

Chorus

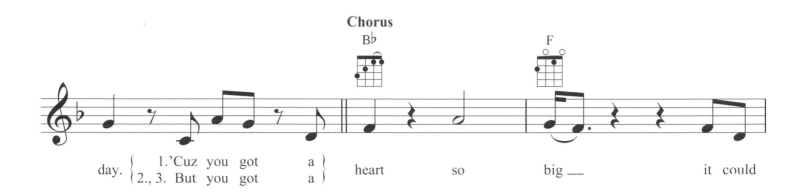

day. { 1.'Cuz you got a } heart so big __ it could

crush this town. And I can't hold _____ out for-

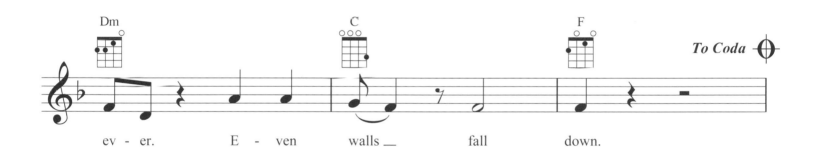

ev - er. E - ven walls __ fall down.

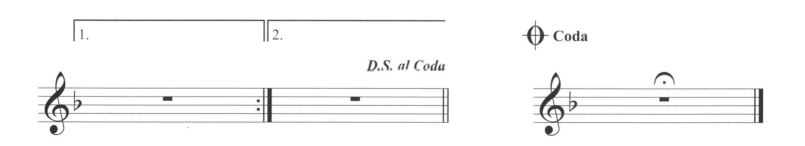

D.S. al Coda

Additional Lyrics

2. All around your island, there's a barricade
   That keeps out the danger and holds in the pain.
   Sometimes you're happy, sometimes you cry.
   Half of me is ocean, half of me is sky.

3. Some things are over, and some things go on.
   Part of me you carry, and part of me is gone.

Wildflowers

Words and Music by Tom Petty

Chorus

who com - pares _____ with you. You be - long _____ a -
You be - long in _ that home by and by. You be - long _____ a -

mong the _ wild - flow - ers. _ You be - long in a boat out at sea.
mong the _ wild - flow - ers. _ You be - long some - where close to me.

To Coda ⊕

You be - long with your love on your arm. _ You be - long some - where
Far a - way from your trou - ble and wor - ry, you be - long some - where

D.S. al Coda   ⊕ **Coda**

you feel _ free.   you feel _ free.

You be - long some - where you feel _____ free.

You Don't Know How It Feels

Words and Music by Tom Petty

You Got Lucky

Words and Music by Tom Petty and Mike Campbell

Chorus

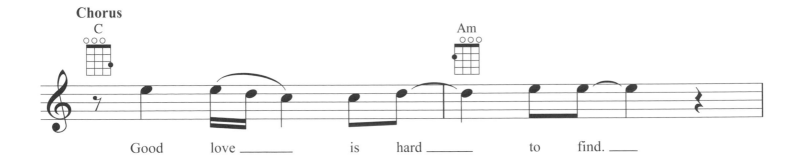

Good love _____ is hard _____ to find. _____

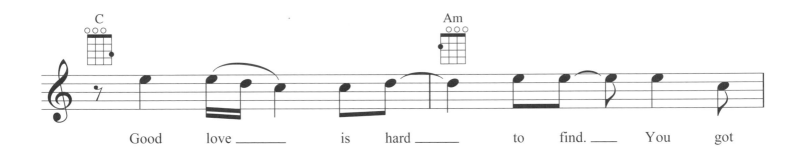

Good love _____ is hard _____ to find. _____ You got

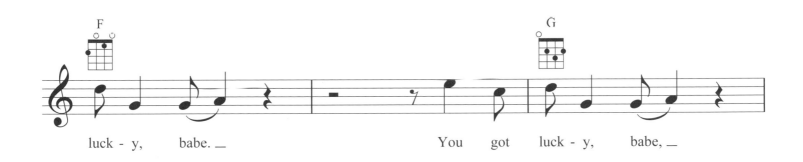

luck - y, babe. _ You got luck - y, babe, _

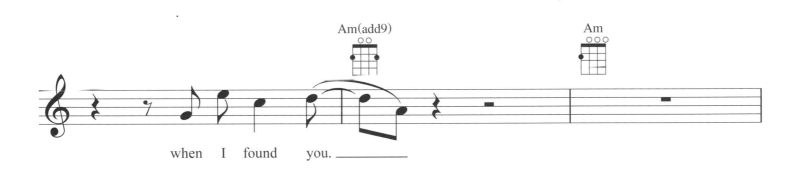

when I found you. _____

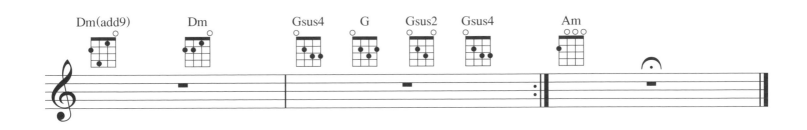

The Waiting

Words and Music by Tom Petty

1. Oh, ba - by, don't it feel like heav - en right now? Don't it
(2.) *See additional lyrics*

feel like some - thing from a dream? __ Yeah, __

I've nev - er known noth - in' quite like this. Don't it feel like to - night might

nev - er be a - gain? Ba - by, we know __ bet - ter than to

try and pre - tend. Hon - ey, no one could - 've ev - er

Don't let it kill you, ba-by. Don't let it get to you. I'll be your bleed-ing heart.

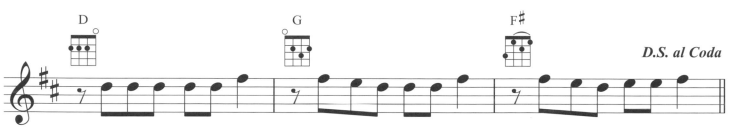

I'll be your cry-in' fool. Don't let this go too far. Don't let it get to you.

D.S. al Coda

Coda

Outro

Yeah, the wait - ing is the

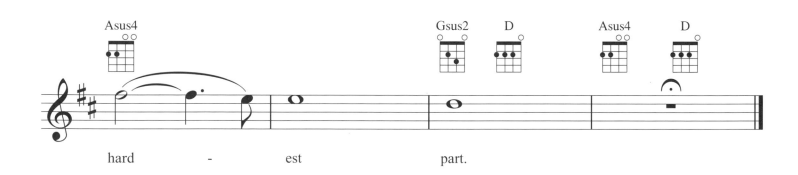

hard - est part.

Additional Lyrics

2. Well, yeah, I might have chased a couple women around.
   All it ever got me was down.
   Yeah, then there were those that made me feel good,
   But never as good as I'm feeling right now.
   Baby, you're the only one that's ever known how
   To make me wanna live like I wanna live now.
   I said, yeah, yeah. (Yeah, yeah.)
   Yeah, yeah, yeah, yeah.